# STAY WOKE, KIDS!

## KAZVARE

CANONGATE

First published in Great Britain in 2021 by Canongate Books Ltd,
14 High Street, Edinburgh EH1 1TE

canongate.co.uk

1

*British Library Cataloguing*-in-Publication Data
A catalogue record for this book is available on
request from the British Library

ISBN 978 1 83885 355 6

Printed and bound in China

KIDS, THIS IS FOR YOU
XO

# I.
# TAKEOVER

# BOW DOWN

Immigrants are taking our jobs!
No wait, all immigrants are slobs!
But when we move countries
We don't give a monkey's –
We're expats, we're awesome, we're gods!

8

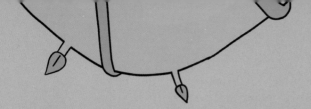

# MINE

Thank God for Kim K and Columbus –
Pioneers, explorers, discoverers!
Whether countries or braids,
They hog accolades
In books and on magazine covers.

# LISTEN

You can sing along with mighty vigour
And spit lyrics with all of the rigour
Of a rapper from Queens
But that doesn't mean
If you're white, you can say
YO! MY N—

# UPGRADE U

Bit rough round the edges they'd say
And then came the big chain café
The next thing you knew
Whole Foods moved in too.
No more food deserts – hip hip *hooray*?

# II.
# HARD KNOCK LIFE

# 1+1

On many boards, there is a ration.
Diversity isn't a passion,
At very most you'll see
One brown face, maybe three?
Tokenism – but make it fashun.

# PARTY

She grew up on three estate blocks,
A small fact that often drew shocks.
"But you speak really well!
You just never could tell!"
She wished that they'd go and kick rocks.

# FORMATION

If you are not white, it's a shame
For you must be lumped in as the same.
Although this sounds wild
It's your destiny, child,
You are BAME, say your name, say your name!

# III.
# EXCUSE ME, MISS

# YES

We know you might be a real rusher
To kiss and to hold and to touch her.
But did she say yes?
If not, do regress –
You don't want confessions, like Usher.

# IF I WERE A BOY

The wish to change the status quo
At times appears so very low.

For does Jade receive
The same wage as Steve?
The answer is L-O-L, no.

# I CARE

She broke her leg and was in pain.
"I think it's most likely a sprain,"
He said without checking
– How very perplexing –
And prescribed her a glass of champagne.

# BONNIE & CLYDE

"If you can't cook, how will he eat?"
My aunt asked, her tone so upbeat.
Amazed by her question
I made the suggestion:
"If he learns to hunt,
we'll be sweet."

# IV.
# THINGS THAT U DO

# FEVER

He never would talk about systems
But always found time to blame victims.
"Me, a racist?!" he cries —
A claim he denies
Despite showing all of the symptoms.

# HOLD UP

"I don't see colour!" she'll yell.
Yet her clothes match impeccably well,
She stops at red lights,
Culls her pinks from her whites,
But with humans? She just cannot tell.

WHAT A BEAUTIFUL BLUE SKY! NOT A CLOUD IN SIGHT.

# CREOLE

If you have at least one good black pal,
Love *Lion King*, have toured Senegal?
You cannot be racist.
Plus 'Pac's on your playlist?
Move on over, *Rachel Dolezal*.

# V.
# EMPIRE STATE OF MIND

# NO ANGEL

There once was a woman
called Jane
Who thought she could
heal all Black pain.
"I have come to save you!"
*Sweetie, we don't need you,*
*Nor one more white*
*saviour campaign.*

WHO IS THIS
WOMAN?

# PARTITION

The system works perfectly fine.
For only a few get to shine.
And so then the rest,
Who aren't hashtag blessed,
Get to twerk on the poverty line.

# SUPERPOWER

There was a young man from a village.
His ancestors, how they did pillage
Lands that weren't theirs,
Passed the gold to their heirs –
But still he denies his white privilege.

# ALL NIGHT

Must be nice to relax in your bed
And nod off despite the bloodshed
By police and the prisons
Inflicted on millions
Of Black men – nighty night, sleepy head.

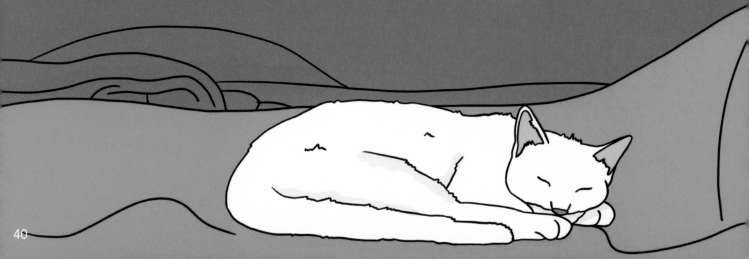

# VI.
# A STAR IS BORN

# BEAUTIFUL LIAR

You could say her world came undone
Straight after that "slip of the tongue",
But don't fear, she'll be fine,
Tears erase any crime.
From "Cancelled" to "U OK, hun?"

# TELEPHONE

Is there anything she won't destroy?
Making calls (that's her ultimate ploy)
To the boys in blue.

"Help! A barbecue!
I spot seasoning! Worst of all – joy!"

# SPEECHLESS

A true ally she nimbly did feign
But her mask slipped, exposing disdain.
Can this really be true?
We were rooting for you!
But don't come to the cookout again.

# DADDY LESSONS

Over this point, sweetheart,
I won't gloss,
For this you must say when you're cross.
So now after three,
Repeat after me:
"I demand to speak to your boss."